Sangre de Cristo
Wilderness

A Territory of the Heart

Photography by

Bob Thomason

Written by

Mary Jean Porter

Music Mountain Press
Westcliffe, Colorado

Sangre de Cristo Wilderness
A Territory of the Heart

ISBN 0-9656126-6-X
First Edition

Copyright
Photography © 1997 Bob Thomason
Text © 1997 Mary Jean Porter

No part of this book may be reproduced in any form without written permission from the publisher with the exception of book reviewers who may quote brief passages or reprint a photograph. Printed in Singapore.

Acknowledgements
We would like to thank the following people for their assistance in the production of this book: Cindy Rivera, district ranger for the U.S. Forest Service's San Carlos District and her dedicated staff; the Forest Service's San Juan Design Team; Hal and Mary Walter for the use of their pack burros, Hannibal and Virgil; Paul Brown of Wet Mountain Llamas for the use of Tommy and Tenzing; bison wranglers Lynn Attebery and Dennis Shaydak.

Special thanks to our wilderness companions:
Patricia Perkinson, Bernie Abrahams, David Purnell, Todd Lloyd, Bryce Lloyd, David Strobel, Brock Henderson, Del Paulson, Rob Gilchrist, Jake Berryhill, Gary Faulkenberry and Michael O' Hanlon.

Music Mountain Press
Box 899
Westcliffe, Colorado 81252

Voice and fax: 719 783-9012
E-mail: tpinc@rmi.net

*Dedicated to the memory of my
mother and father
and to my wife Patricia*

Dedicated to Bernie and Della Abrahams

Table of Contents

Introduction — 5

The Sangre de Cristo Wilderness — 9

A Territory of the Heart — 15

Notes — 48

Bison herd on the Shaydak Ranch, with the Sangre de Cristo Mountains in the background.

Introduction

Today is the first day of winter, and from my home in Westcliffe I can see the snow-capped peaks and passes of the Sangre de Cristo Wilderness. At midmorning it is 30°F and the wind is gusting 30 to 40 miles per hour. On a day like this, one needs only to step outside for a moment to understand the challenges faced by the area's native people and those first pioneers. The wilderness was all around them. Their challenge was not to tame the land because that is clearly impossible, but rather to adapt themselves to the land and understand how best to use its resources.

The people of today have a wilderness challenge, too. It is no less daunting a task than that which faced the pioneers and it also is fraught with difficulty and uncertainty. Our challenge — understanding how best to preserve the wilderness for future generations — is great enough to test anyone who enjoys wild lands.

The word "exploration" does not have the same meaning it once had. Today we have accurate maps, and high-tech camping gear. But there are still great adventures to be had in these mountains. Perhaps today it is an inward journey — a journey to explore ourselves as much as to explore uncharted lands.

In this collection of photographs of the Sangre de Cristo Wilderness, I am on both an inward and outward journey. I want to use equal parts of my emotion, mind and muscle to explore this place. For me photography is about creating images that have a roundness and fullness to them — images that express this inward and outward exploration.

Mary Jean Porter is on a similar journey. She knows that wilderness has the power to renew the human spirit. And in her essay "A Territory of the Heart" she creates word images with such clarity and depth that readers may take this wilderness experience with them wherever they may go.

This book has been a labor of love — we hope you enjoy it as much as we have enjoyed bringing it to you.

Bob Thomason

The Wet Mountain Valley and the Sangre de Cristo Mountains during late summer.

Humboldt Peak, Crestone Needle and Crestone Peak at sunrise

The Sangre de Cristo Wilderness

The Sangre de Cristo Wilderness Area, 226,455 acres of mountains in south-central Colorado, was set aside by Congress in the 1993 Colorado Wilderness Act. The act designated approximately 611,730 new acres of wilderness in the state. Nine new wilderness areas were created — the Sangre de Cristo was by far the largest — and acreage was added to nine existing areas.

The 70-mile-long wilderness area takes its name from the Sangre de Cristo mountain range where it is located. The Spanish words mean "blood of Christ," and legend says they describe the mountains' reddish glow at sunrise and sunset.

The mountains rise abruptly from the Wet Mountain Valley on the east and from the San Luis Valley on the west. The wilderness area runs along the crest of the range and part way down the mountains on both sides. The Great Sand Dunes National Monument is adjacent to the southern part of the wilderness area, on the San Luis Valley side, and the Arkansas River flows a few miles beyond the wilderness' northern boundary.

The long, narrow wilderness area is breached by two four-wheel drive roads — Hayden Pass in the north and Medano Pass in the south. Private land around Lily Lake near Blanca Peak creates another division in the wilderness.

The Rainbow Trail skirts the eastern edge of the wilderness at an average elevation of 9,000 feet, providing access to other trails that follow drainages up into the mountains. Many trails also follow creeks up the western flank of the Sangre de Cristos from the San Luis Valley into the wilderness area.

Hiking these trails, a visitor is likely to see small animals like chipmunks and squirrels and a variety of small birds. But the wilderness area also is home to black bear, mule deer and elk, bighorn sheep, mountain lions, porcupines, coyotes, beavers, marmots, martens and pikas, and to larger birds such as wild turkeys, jays, hawks and owls.

Piñon and ponderosa pines, juniper, gambel oak, mountain mahogany and cottonwoods grow at lower elevations, followed by lodgepole pine, aspen, Engelmann spruce and subalpine fir in higher areas. Wind-tortured bristlecone pines and Engelmann spruce grow near timberline.

The forests, meadows and creek banks of the wilderness area are filled with flowers, including Colorado's own beautiful blue columbine. Others are lupine, cinquefoil, arnica, many species of aster, buttercup, Indian paintbrush, little red elephants, brook primrose, harebell, larkspur, wild geranium and the lovely but deadly monkshood, also known as wolfbane or aconite.

Frosty ball or alpine thistle — one of the strangest flowers you'll ever encounter — bistort, arctic gentian, speedwell, moss campion and others grow at 10,000 feet and above, near glacier-sculpted lakes and the rubble left by rock slides.

The steep, rugged Sangre de Cristos didn't need official designation to be considered wild land, says Mike Smith of the U.S. Forest Service's San Carlos District.

"They were a de facto wilderness that we recognized with designation."

That doesn't mean the Sangre de Cristos were untouched. For centuries, man has ventured into the mountains in search of food or precious metals, to cut wood or graze stock. Evidence of these activities can be seen in Indian artifacts, and in old cabins, mine dumps and piles of rusted cans. Man's recent presence in the area is more graphically recorded in blazed and initial-scarred aspen trees.

The Sangre de Cristo Wilderness Area was carved from the San Isabel and Rio Grande National Forests, although some of it was Bureau of Land Management land. It falls within four ranger districts — the San Carlos, Salida, Saguache and Conejos Peak — but the forest service manages it as a single unit.

Like all wilderness in Colorado, the Sangre de Cristo is managed under the national Wilderness Act of 1964, which established areas "where the earth and its community of life are untrammeled by man, where man himself is a visitor who does not remain."

Regulations allow visitors to hike, backpack, cross-country ski, snowshoe, ride a horse or take a wheelchair into the wilderness area, but not drive a motorized vehicle, ride a bike, hang-glide or use a chainsaw. Aircraft are allowed only in some emergencies.

Visitors may collect rocks by non-mechanical means, but they may not collect plants and they are forbidden to remove or deface archaeological, historical or paleontological remains. Hunting, fishing and non-commercial trapping are allowed under state laws.

Mountains make the Sangre de Cristo Wilderness Area — sharp, blue mountains marching northwest to southeast across the tawny landscape.

One after another the mountains pierce the sky at 12,000, 13,000 and more than 14,000 feet. They rear up from the Wet Mountain and the San Luis valley floors and gain as much as 7,000 feet in elevation.

Because of this, they offer steep trails and magnificent scenery. Few Colorado mountain ranges present the heart-stopping panorama that the Sangre de Cristos do.

The Sangres are a fault block range. Millions of years ago, the peaks were pushed up through faults in the earth at the eastern edge of the San Luis Valley. They later were eroded by glaciers.

Although eight mountains in the Sangre de Cristos are more than 14,000 feet in elevation and considered official "Fourteeners," only four are included in the wilderness area: Crestone Peak (14,294 feet), Crestone Needle (14,197 feet), Kit Carson (14,165 feet) and Humboldt (14,064 feet). Crestone is the seventh-highest mountain in Colorado. Crestone Needle is No. 20, Kit Carson is No. 23, and Humboldt is No. 37.

The Crestones may have taken their names from the Spanish word *creston*, which means cockscomb. Kit Carson was named for the Kentucky-born scout, trapper and trader who made a name for himself in the West. Humboldt probably was named for geographer and climber Alexander von Humboldt.

Parry's primrose and other wildflowers carpet the western slope of Humboldt Peak in August. Crestone Needle (14,197 feet) and Crestone Peak (14,294 feet) rise in the background, attracting climbers from around the world. Despite the dismal state of the four-wheel drive access road, South Colony drainage is one of the most heavily used in the Sangres.

The names of at least two other mountains in the wilderness area — Mount Niehardt and Milwaukee Peak — also reflect the German heritage of the Wet Mountain Valley. DeAnza Peak, Rito Alto Peak, Pico Aislado and Tijeras Peak reflect the Spanish presence in the Sangre de Cristos, and Comanche Peak reminds us that Indians once lived in this part of Colorado.

Many mountains are named for people — Simmons, Bushnell, Gibbs, Owen, Gibson, Marcy and Adams — and some like Cottonwood, Huckleberry, Blueberry, Sheep and Spread Eagle, for plants and animals.

There are mountains with wonderfully descriptive names like Blizzardine, Nipple, Thirsty, Electric, Eureka and Music, and there are the more pedestrian Red Mountain and Black Mountain.

One peak, Challenger, honors the astronauts who died in the 1986 space shuttle explosion. It is a subpeak of Kit Carson.

It seems fitting that at least one mountain in the wilderness area honors Americans who died in pursuit of a dream because mountains always have inspired dreams. Like wilderness, they represent our fondest hopes for ourselves. Going into them, we seek wealth, strength, beauty, enlightenment, peace.

Mountains challenge the body, please the eye, nourish the spirit.

To a girl growing up on the flat, hot Southern Colorado prairie, the Sangre de Cristos were an exotic paradise — a cool blue dream of wildflowers and dancing water and shy fawns.

Although many of the people who visit the wilderness area today undoubtedly would express less romantic sentiments, I think they feel the same way. Unless we live in the midst of the mountains, they stand in dramatic contrast to our daily surroundings. They are extraordinary, and we can't help but set them apart in our thoughts.

Wilderness designation set the Sangre de Cristos apart in reality. It would be a cruel irony if, in seeking to preserve what is best about the mountains, we have drawn attention to them that eventually will lead to their ruin.

Let us hope that while calling these beautiful mountains "wilderness," we can save what makes them special to each of us. The Sangres deserve to remain as splendid as they are today, and our grandchildren and great-grandchildren deserve their chance to appreciate them.

Patricia Perkinson and Virgil on the Goodwin Lakes Trail (top left). Patricia wading across the mouth of Upper Macey Lake (top right). Jake Berryhill and Hannibal climbing the Stout Creek Lakes Trail (bottom right). Patricia and Hannibal in a meeting of minds (bottom left).

Alpine groundsel and purple subalpine daisies near Upper Sand Creek Lake

A Territory of the Heart

Wilderness. A place apart. A cathedral where the sky sweeps down to meet the earth, where rivers born of frozen lakes start their journeys to the sea, where centuries or seconds pass the same in the slow, uncaring cycles that govern nature.

Wilderness. A refuge for plants and animals where life can flourish undisturbed by man and his developments. A "savage" land beyond the civilizing influences of humanity.

Wilderness. A place that existed long before us and will exist long after. A place that has no use for us, but which we need for many reasons. The place from which we came.

Wilderness. A haven of solitude and peace, an antidote for the stresses of 20th-century life. A place where the only wars are fought between the elements, where the only schedules are the ones we impose upon ourselves, and the only clocks are the sun and the seasons.

Wilderness. A place of breathtaking beauty — enough to feed the soul for a lifetime, to inspire poets and painters, hunters and hikers, to reward earthly man and woman with a glimpse of heaven.

Wilderness. A territory of the heart.

The Sangre de Cristo Wilderness Area in south-central Colorado is all of these and much more. It is as simple and beautiful as the five-petaled wild rose that grows along the edges of its meadows, as complex as the debate about how America's public lands should be managed.

Running along the crest and down the slopes of the Sangre de Cristo mountain range, the wilderness area attracts residents from the valleys on either side — people who consider it "home" because they grew up hiking or hunting in the mountains, or because their families once cut wood or grazed their sheep or cattle there.

People also come from nearby cities like Pueblo and Colorado Springs, from more distant places like Denver and Boulder, from other states. They come for a day, or to spend a long holiday weekend, or to hike for a week up and down the area's steep trails. They come to climb a "Fourteener" or two, to fish in a shade-dappled pool, to ski or snowshoe quiet miles through a forest-turned-fairyland, to see the wildflowers or the aspens at their most vivid.

They take photos or write poems or paint pictures to match their dreams.

They eat squashed sandwiches and reconstituted "backpacker" dinners and they drink lousy cowboy coffee. They endure soggy socks, sunburned and windburned faces, ticks, mosquitoes, ants, blisters, rain, hail, snow and wind, and sometimes leaky tents and stony ground.

They come in all seasons, in all weather, even when common sense should keep them at home. They come to the wilderness area because they can't stay away.

What lures them, what siren whispers her song of beauty, mystery and pleasure?

The reasons might be as individual as visitors' names, but I believe many people come to the Sangre de Cristo Wilderness Area, to any wild place, because they seek a connection with something greater than themselves — the natural world, spirit, God; call it what you like.

I think they want to spend time in a quiet, beautiful, often lonely place so they can feel what it really means to be alive, what it means to exist, however briefly, in a world that hasn't been significantly changed by man.

I think people want to realize — at a level deeper than the intellectual — that a spring-fed lake high in the mountains is where their water actually comes from; that berries, rosehips, acorns, grass seeds, fish and "wild animals" provide food more basic than a supermarket; that, as human beings, a wild place truly is their birthplace even though they were born in hospitals and their ancestors might have lived in cities.

Wilderness is at the root of our lives. It is the home, the reunion we yearn for when we watch a sunset and feel heartache. It is the past we try to recreate in our movies about wild times on a frontier peopled by cowboys and Indians — no matter how grim the reality might have been. It is the reason we make heroes of our explorers and astronauts.

Our wilderness connection is why a book about "running with the wolves" became an overnight best seller and why the coyote — a creature feared, despised, reduced to fur collars — is an icon of popular culture. Coyote is wild, unpredictable and does what it pleases. Don't we wish the same for ourselves?

That we revere wilderness can be seen in our determined effort to save the bald eagle, our national bird, from extinction and in our delight at seeing one today. It can be seen in vacationers paying thousands of dollars for the privilege of watching whales or zebras in the wild, or for a raft trip down a rampaging river, or a visit to a Central American jungle.

Wilderness represents what we human beings already have lost of our birthright, the natural world, and what remains. It represents our past and our future, our heritage and our legacy.

Aspen forest near treeline on the San Isabel Creek Trail

Aspen Trees in Winter

Pilgrims

To this wilderness of lichened slopes
windswept bristlecone and purple aconite
we come as visitors,
our heads checked at the box below
where we signed our names,
our hearts in our hands
on our sleeves
in the pockets of the flannel shirts we wear.
These hearts are our guides.
They will teach us what books cannot
about this windy peak
this sky that streaks above us
this field of alpine strawberries
with fruit like tiny rubies.
Our hearts will teach us
what more knowledgeable men and women cannot
about this special place.
They are all we need to appreciate this wilderness.
They are the wild parts of us —
the perfect match for this wild place.

Wilderness is as it always has been, ever since life was set in motion. It is fluid like the waters of one of its creeks, graceful like the sway of a sapling in the breeze. And when we visit, wilderness lends this fluidity and grace to our lives. It blesses us. It takes us out of ourselves and gives us new perspectives. It humbles, awes and inspires us with its power and its grandeur and its beauty. It is a gift that enriches and enhances our lives.

We may gain a sense of its spirit from the many artists and writers who have tried to define it, but we don't really taste the essence of wilderness until we walk beneath a canopy of golden aspens, or lie in a meadow of wildflowers and pick out shapes in the clouds that float above, or hear thunder and its echo in a rocky bowl above timberline, or shiver in the cold wind of a mountaintop and watch the play of light and shadow on the world below.

An hour spent in wilderness is restorative in ways that health-club workouts, alcohol or prescription drugs, most stress-reduction techniques never can be because wilderness touches the soul and the heart.

And if we can't always experience wilderness firsthand, we can know it exists and be comforted by that knowledge. I might only see it once, but I know that an icy lake high against the sky catches the colors of sunrise and sunset, and that a patch of fuchsia shooting stars blooms beside a waterfall. I know that Amanita muscaria grows like a blood-red surprise on the forest floor, and that Steller's jays flash through the trees.

And in my mind and heart I can retreat to those places, those snapshots of beauty, whenever I wish.

I earn my living at a computer terminal in a 9-to-5 job, so wilderness is more dream than reality for me, but that makes it no less precious.

It is a dream that consoles me on long afternoons when the phone keeps ringing, the clock ticks faster and my deadline looms. It is a dream that helps me keep balance in a world that's changing too quickly for my taste, a world that seems increasingly violent and preoccupied with nonsense.

This wilderness dream helps define who I am. I might participate in and have the trappings of modern, middle-class life, but part of me is "checked out." I feel different — I am different — because I have been to the wild. I have seen its great beauty, heard its silence, felt its solitude, magic and mystery, and I cherish them. Long ago, the natural world branded my heart and claimed my allegiance.

I don't think I'm special because I feel this way, and I know I'm not alone in these kinds of feelings. Wilderness appreciation is not an exclusive club — it is open to everyone.

I think a lot of wilderness designation involves the specialness to the people," says Cindy Rivera, district ranger for the U.S. Forest Service's San Carlos District. "It takes a certain amount of public support to get Congress to support designation in the first place.

"Most of the value of wilderness to me is intangible, spiritual, and knowing the lands are protected forever. The Sangres are a place to go out and see nature's beauty and freedom of spirit and get that uplift that only nature can give.

"My background is outdoor recreation management, and the opportunity to go out and recreate is important. But when it comes to recreation and getting into the outdoors, there are so many places you can go besides wilderness.

"The vastness, the solitude, the fact that it is protected all make wilderness special," Rivera says.

Doug Cain agrees, but has different reasons. A Puebloan who has a cabin north of Westcliffe, near the Rainbow Trail, he has hiked the Sangre de Cristos in all seasons and has skied and snowshoed there in winter. He says the quiet and the beauty of the wilderness area are what make it a special place.

"Nature's beauty is always more impressive than man's creations," says Cain, a hydrologist for the U.S. Geological Survey. "The wilderness area is a place to go to get centered, to be calm and quiet and to listen, to let a lot of the noise of the world go.

"One of my favorite environments is alpine tundra in the summer. Sometimes what I'll try to do in the middle of the hustle and bustle of daily existence is to summon up those places. Even if I couldn't go there for some reason, it would still exist for me.

Swift Creek beaver ponds below Lake of the Clouds

Boulder field at 11,500 feet in Texas Creek drainage

"Even if you've never been there, it still seems like it's important that there are places that are wild and free and unspoiled.

"The Sangres are special in another way," Cain says. "They are so high and steep, there are so many lakes and streams. To be on one of the peaks and look down this long string of mountains — it's just mountain after mountain."

Writer Hal Walter, who lives in the Wet Mountains but often hikes, skis, camps, hunts and fishes in the Sangre de Cristos, says the wilderness area is special because it can't easily be exploited.

"People have tried to log it, to mine it, to recreate in it, but there are no minerals, logging is marginal, skiing is too difficult. In other places, you can drive to where you want to ski; here, you're looking at walking through mud to get up high enough to showshoe or cross-country ski," he says.

"In this day and age, when everything is bottom line, a wilderness area is not profitable for anybody. Maybe because wilderness is the only thing not controlled by business interests, it is the only thing we can stand up for and save as a society."

Walter reconsiders, then adds: "People are exploiting these mountains in one way — the outdoor industry. The mountains are a place to use outdoor gear. As a result, the lakes are like little sacrifice areas. Everyone makes them their destination."

He says wilderness is important because it provides a place for animals to live.

He also says it is part of our identity as Americans.

"The whole idea of discovering a new continent and traveling across it is part of who we are. The idea that we left a little bit of what was here when we found it is important.

"If you were to go into the Sangres and all there was was condos and strip mines, what would that say about us as a society?

"Americans want wilderness," Walter says.

"Whether you go to visit, or it's just a place in your head, it's a comforting thought."

Mike Smith, a forest service employee who is coordinator for the Sangre de Cristo Wilderness Area, echoes the frontier theme.

"Wilderness is one of the last places where you can live out the American dream, the American heritage. It is one of the last areas where you can experience an encounter with the frontier spirit.

"The frontier experience identifies Americans for what we are. It's part of our culture — the hope of doing something better. Wilderness areas symbolize hope in some way — hope for what we find in ourselves, hope that some of the earth remains unmanaged, hope for society that these areas remain.

"People who never visit wilderness like the idea that these areas still exist. It inspires people that there are wild areas."

Smith calls this knowledge "the wild dream."

He says solitude is another important aspect of wilderness.

"Solitude is an increasing rarity as we become closer together. Hermits and Jesus Christ and people for thousands of years have looked at solitude as a tool. It allows us to put things into perspective.

"You feel insignificant. It clarifies what's really important. Some of the things that seem like big problems aren't so significant.

"It's like going to a third world country — it changes your perspective," Smith says.

Mike O'Hanlon, a Rosita resident who has hiked and backpacked in the Sangre de Cristos for more than 20 years, calls the mountains "my sanity place. A place to go up in to hike, to put in perspective all the stresses of the day."

He is author of *The Colorado Sangre de Cristo: A Complete Trail Guide,* and is a member of the Custer (County) Search and Rescue group, activities which have added to his knowledge and broadened his view of the mountains.

Although he clearly values wilderness, he is reluctant to say what makes it special.

"I see it in almost a metaphysical way," O'Hanlon says. "The value and the essence that's there is beyond words. The more you try to put it in words, the more it gets away from you.

"There is a huge genre of literature today, and has been for the past 150 years, where people have gone into the wilderness and tried to write about it. The quandary becomes the old classic dilemma of trying to grab the reflection in the pond with your hands. The best nature writers fully appreciate that dilemma.

"There's something there for me, but I don't want them to put it into words for me, and I don't want to try to myself."

Christine Cloninger is a wilderness back-country ranger for the forest service, whose job includes educating people about "leaving no trace" on the Sangres wilderness area. She also samples lakes for evidence of acid rain. From the back of her horse, Cloninger gains a slightly different perspective of the Sangre de Cristos.

"To me, what wilderness means is a place we want to preserve for our future generations. I think it's important to preserve it for our kids.

"Just a pristine place — that's what wilderness means."

Wilderness is set aside for practical reasons, too. It provides a place for plants and animals to live, where their genes can be preserved yet new genes can enter. It provides science with "living laboratories" where these plants and animals and their relationships to each other and the environment can be studied. And it offers a treasure trove of resources — potential cures for life-threatening illnesses. Wilderness provides a bench mark against which the developed world can be measured. We can see just how far we have come, for better or worse.

Goodwin Lake after a summer hailstorm.

Silence

*Silence fills this sacred place
like the space between heartbeats
the pause between breaths.
It presses my ear
like the swish of the sea
caught in the whorls of a shell.*

*A companion
like the pulse of blood
at my throat
a witness to my thoughts
a canvas for my brush
of sighs or screams or prayers,
silence is.*

It is, it is.

Clouds blanket the Wet Mountain Valley. Sunrise reflected in Goodwin Lake (facing page).

Aspen trees, a member of the poplar family, are generally found at altitudes of 10,000 to 11,000 feet on both north- and south-facing slopes. The structure of the leaf stem allows the leaves of the 'quaking' aspen to easily move from side to side but not up and down. Triggered by shorter mid-September days, aspen trees along North Taylor Creek Trail (above) and North Crestone Lake Trail (right) show their colors. Autumn sunset paints Spring Mountain and the Wet Mountain Valley (facing page).

Autumn colors at 11,000 feet on North Crestone Lake Trail

Lush green moss covers rocks of Stout Creek (facing page and right) where it crosses the Stout Creek Trail at about 9,500 feet. A cutthroat trout (above) swims in the cold, clear waters of North Taylor Creek.

An afternoon thunderstorm (above) rolls over the crest of the Sangres into the Texas Creek drainage. The west side of a bristlecone pine (facing page) shows the effects of the prevailing westerly wind at 12,300 feet. A band of bark indicates the tree's living tissue.

A female Rocky Mountain sheep and her young (above) shed their winter coats. Boulder fields like this one at Upper Macey Lake provide prime habitat for sheep and a canvas for lichens. Dual organisms composed of a fungus and an alga, lichens (facing page) thrive in cold, dry and unpolluted mountain air.

Upper Macey Lake at 11,865 feet

Snow

It snows tonight
the first snow of the year
silver streaks beyond the black glass
of my room.

I remember other snows
how they caught the scrub oak by surprise
how the aspen and the asters
were startled by the white,
how the winter woods were silenced
and the landscape lullabied
by snow.
I remember pale pasque flowers
violet against spring snow,
globeflower, marsh marigold
pushing through the dirtywhite
snow-becoming-water
trickling to the sea.
I remember snow on peaks
in never-summer couloirs
when snow was but a memory
below.

Outside my window
the snow piles up
making icy spikes of still-green grass.
Too early
for this weather,
but a circle has no breaks —
fall-winter-spring-summer snow —
and 'early' has no meaning
for these silver flakes.

Frozen Medano Creek (left) in January. By mid-summer of most years, the creek has diminished to a trickle or dried up entirely before reaching the Great Sand Dunes National Monument. The dunes, another wilderness area separate from the Sangre de Cristo Wilderness, are the tallest sand dunes in North America. They reach nearly 750 feet in height, cover approximately 39 square miles, and were formed by winds that sweep across the San Luis Valley. The billions of grains of sand that form the dunes originally were deposited on the valley floor by the Rio Grande River. Winds blowing to the northeast pushed the sand until it was caught by the barrier of the Sangre de Cristo Mountains (above). Over thousands of years, the sand piled up into dunes at the base of the mountains. The wind that created the dunes constantly reshapes them, carving new patterns into their crystalline surface and sculpting new ridges and hollows.

Sangre de Cristo Wilderness with the Great Sand Dunes National Monument in the foreground at sunset

The Colorado columbine (top), growing near Goodwin Lake, first was identified by Edwin James in 1820 and became the state flower of Colorado in 1899. Fireweed and dwarf goldenweed (above), near treeline in the Texas Creek drainage. Pyxie cup or goblet lichen (right), about one inch high, growing on rocks in Big Cottonwood Creek. Throughout the Sangres, water from melting snow flows through lakes, streams and cascades like Macey Falls (facing page) and replenishes the aquifers of the San Luis and Wet Mountain valleys.

North Crestone Lake at 11,750 feet is the largest lake in the Sangre de Cristo Wilderness

The Authors

Bob Thomason received a bachelor of fine arts degree from Florida State University where he studied photography, music composition and art history.

He has been a commercial photographer for 20 years. His photography covers many subjects and has been published worldwide in books, magazines and advertising.

He and his wife, Patricia Perkinson, live in Westcliffe, Colorado.

Mary Jean Porter has been a feature writer for the Pueblo Chieftain for 20 years, covering the arts, education and the outdoors. She earned a bachelor's degree in anthropology from the University of Colorado at Boulder.

Her poetry has been published by the Pueblo Poetry Project in a chapbook and in several anthologies.

She lives with her family in Custer County, Colorado.

The Photographs

The panorama photographs (2 page spreads) were produced with a Fuji G617 panorama camera.

Other images were made with a Nikon F4 camera and Nikkor lenses with focal lengths from 20mm to 300mm.

All of the images in the book were produced on Fuji Velvia film.

Signed limited-edition prints and posters of selected photographs are available by contacting Music Mountain Press.

Bibliography

Guennel, G. K., *Guide to Colorado Wildflowers*, (Englewood, CO: Westcliffe, 1995)

O'Hanlon, Michael, *The Colorado Sangre de Cristo: A Complete Trail Guide*, (Westcliffe, CO: Hungry Gulch Press, 1996)

Pearson, Mark, *The Complete Guide to Colorado's Wilderness Areas*, (Englewood, CO: Westcliffe, 1994)

Shuttleworth, Floyd S. Ph.D, *Non-Flowering Plants*, (New York, NY: Golden Press, 1967)

Skiff, Carl, ed., *The Majestic Fourteeners*, (Silverton, CO: Sundance, 1977)

Weber, William A., *Colorado Flora, Eastern Slope*, (Niwot, CO: University Press of Colorado, 1990)

Further Information

Salida Ranger District (east side of the wilderness area, north of Hayden Pass) 325 W. Rainbow Blvd., Salida, CO 81201, Phone (719) 539-3591.

San Carlos Ranger District (east side, south of Hayden Pass) 3170 E. Main Street, Cañon City, CO 81212, Phone (719) 269-8500.

Saguache Ranger District (west side, north of Medano Pass) Box 67, Saguache, CO 81149, Phone (719) 655-2547.

Conejos Peak Ranger District (west side, south of Medano Pass) Box 420, La Jara, CO 81140, Phone (719) 274-8971.

Credits

Photography: Bob Thomason
Text: Mary Jean Porter
Book Design: Bob Thomason and Patricia Perkinson
Map Data: U.S. Forest Service's San Juan Design Team
Proofing: Leah Lahtinen

Production Notes

A Gateway 2000 P5-100 computer and QuarkXpress and Adobe Illustrator software were used for book design and layout. Titles are Adobe Copperplate 31ab, body copy is Adobe Optima and Optima Oblique. Printing and manufacturing by Tien Wah Press, Ltd.

To Order Books

To order additional copies of this book please send your name, mailing address and a check for $18.45 (15.95 plus 2.50 shipping and handling) to:

Music Mountain Press
Box 899
Westcliffe, CO 81252

Posters and signed limited-edition prints of selected images are also available. Contact us for more information.

Voice and Fax: (719) 783-9012
Email: tpinc@rmi.net